VOYAGES TO THE INLAND SEA, IV

Fourth in a series on contemporary Midwestern poetry

Voyages to the Inland Sea, IV

Essays and Poems by

Alvin Greenberg—George Chambers—Raymond Roseliep

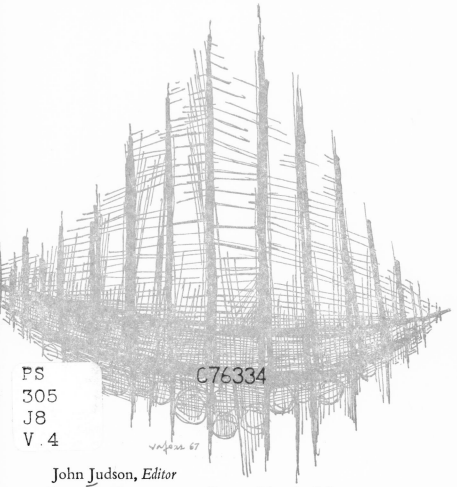

John Judson, *Editor*
Center for Contemporary Poetry, Murphy Library
University of Wisconsin—La Crosse, 1974

INTRODUCTION

A GROUP of grade school children working in a creativity class I co-teach has decided that the *w* in *sword* and the *l* in *could,* letters which we see but which we don't hear, are there because the imagination did it, for the imagination does wondrous things. One might take this assumption and build an analogy to explain the purpose of VOYAGES, and though it may sound strange to East or West Coast ears, it may have a kind of authority and integrity of itself. After all, though the *w* and the *l* are silent, they do significantly help characterize the words they are part of. And after all, maybe that is what many good poets do for the Midwest. VOYAGES is here so that we might see clearly those we don't often get the chance to hear.

Still, a few reviewers and critics of this series contend that it is too regional, and for these the term *regional* means parochial; it has decidedly negative connotations. But it is not our purpose to use their definition, nor to publish the work of poets who strictly support it. As I indicated in the introduction to VOYAGES II, this series is interested in publishing good work by Midwestern poets and in giving each a chance to tell us a bit about himself and the way he sees his world.

The world of "big" publishing being what it is, essentially Eastern in concern and location, and profit oriented, much of what is of value in the Midwest has been neglected because it would not sell in the East. Neither could those publishers imagine a Midwestern audience from which they might profit. Such "big" publishers never seemed to consider that, advertising, fads, and Rod Mc-Kuen aside, economics and mass prestige might not have anything to do with poems or with some poets who write them.

Don't get me wrong. I am not hostile about this or angry. My tone is a bit Midwestern: a bit matter-of-fact and ironic (tinged, I hope, with some suppressed humor) for, in effect, such avoidance by the Eastern spotlight has probably been instrumental in promoting alternate values for Midwestern poets to grow with and to write about. One might ask if Bly or Stafford could have grown poetically, centered about money rather than a Midwestern landscape, or about mass prestige rather than concerns for spirit, compassion, and awe.

This series, however, does not exist to focus on such excellent, widely published poets as these. The series exists to publish excellent Midwestern poets who have not received such national attention. And it is my hope that it will continue to do so and to remain Midwestern in source as well as interest. If it succeeds, it may help prove that to anthologize Midwestern poets is not to publish those who have been deprived or restricted by geography. It may, in fact, prove that the work of our best poets is for us a means of perceiving new spiritual, aesthetic, and cultural truths about ourselves.

John Judson
La Crosse, Wisconsin

POLARITIES

7
Alvin
Greenberg

So OFTEN the poem itself is the best thing one can say about poetry, demonstration of the thesis that every poem is in fact a poem about poetry, not about poetry alone because always (well, almost always) about something substantially else, but about poetry at the same time: the poem itself formulated somewhere between a sense of art as experience and the sense of the experience of one's life, in which the poem is the taking shape of one's perceptions, and by showing that it is possible to give a moving and verbal shape to those otherwise chaotic and inarticulate perceptions says, in effect, Look, this is the way poems are made, this is what poetry is all about. As the committed reader readily understands.

the commuter

for the dreamer among the rapid lanes of traffic
there is no room. for the amateur
drifting casually down the access ramp

no break in the dense flow of imagination.
no chance to squeeze in between the discrete moments
of the possible for the sunday driver,
complacent in his green convertible.

and yet: five days a week, morning and evening,
gliding cool as a critic between the reckless lines
of traffic, creating as he veers into them
the empty spaces in which his life is possible,

the perfect reader of poetry moves among us:

his hands easy on the firm wheel of the object
—and his mind always on survival.

8

Alvin
Greenberg

At times one writes the poem so overtly about poetry ("curb your dog") that the only hope left afterwards is that it's all out of the system and won't soon have to be repeated; at times one writes the poem so overtly about poetry ("miscellaneous landscape") that the only knowledge clear afterwards is that it can't possibly be about poetry after all. As with other polarities, mostly one lives in between these.

✦

Where one lives, of course, is where the poem is. One recalls Wallace Stevens:
> From this the poem springs: that we live in a place
> That is not our own . . .
and writes out of the polarities of belonging/not-belonging. Or make that longing/belonging: poetry meets Novalis' definition of philosophy as "really homesickness: it is the urge to be at home everywhere." Mostly, of course, everywhere that one is not: the poem as an attempt to shape the everywhere/everything into the recognizable design of one's own domicile—knowing all the while, of course, that it's not. Or (Stevens again: the miraculous and ordinary jar), the poem as an attempt to suburbanize the wilderness, struggling to make a comfortable dwelling place where one can't dwell comfortably, building in the very struggle, between those poles, the shape (=the meaning) of one's experience, poem, life. Or vice versa, reforesting the suburbs to make them interesting and liveable: let chaos (one knows it's there, after all) be seen among the ordered stanzas of the neighborhood.

⚵

Shape, shape, shape (chaos, chaos, chaos): as Lukacs says of the novel, "The creation of forms is the most profound confirmation of the existence of a dissonance." The poet as a settler, platting the wilderness of his own existence, laying the grids of poetic shape over rolling hills and ragged shorelines, looking back down the history of explorations, the ways others have done it, inventing shapes where the old ones won't do, finding shapes where invention stutters, but forever shaping, shaping, shaping (always in the midst of chaos, chaos, chaos).

⚵

curb your dog

piss on poetry: it's full of sharp edges,
rusty spikes that can even lead to lockjaw
and thorns too   burrs like those that stick
in dogs' coats   you don't even know they're
there, and when you do and shake them loose
the seed falls on someone else's property.

next spring, it's your fault he has weeds.

⚵

So one seeks to write the poem that will touch another only to be terrified, at times, on finding how deeply one has touched, the unexpected growths that have sprung suddenly up. Well, one has plenty of strange growths oneself and is generally torn between wanting to rid oneself of them and trying to hang on to them in utter fascination. They are not unidentifiable with what one is, are they? Or one simply grows, in strange places: torn again, between the desire to have roots and the need to be cut free from them; or between the desire to maintain one's geographical freedom and the lust for roots. To have a place, as a writer, to be regional in any sense of the word, is meaningless unless one has some sense of where that place is, the context of that region; unless one senses the region itself as significant in terms of its polarity to some larger context, the larger context capable of providing some meaning to that (life or art) to which the region gives form. Or is it the other way around?

⠿

Form and meaning. Technique, one is always hurrying to assert, isn't everything, but without it there's nothing. Literally nothing. One can't write at all without technique, some sort of technique. But the point is, to know the techniques of poetry, to master and be able to use them. There is nothing without technique, just as the message of this freudian century is that there is nothing without meaning: that everything—every action, thought, feeling, dream, incident—no matter how slight, is full of meaning. Is it possible to live with so much meaning, so much knowledge? Therefore, perhaps, one indulges in the quest for the meaningless, the insignificant . . . only to discover that the quest itself is full of meaning. And not without technique. The self, like the poem, emergent among these particulars.

⠿

Ultimately one wants to say:

> This is no poem, friend:
> This is my life.

But it's neither. Or it's both. Wherever it is, one works like hell to get there, never quite sure where it is that one's gotten to but finally alive between the lines, putting in the plumbing, hooking up the wiring (poetry is a *self*-powered mechanism), ever the busy workman whistling that unforgettable tune from Roethke's notebooks:

> Sure I'm crazy
> But it ain't easy

§

"Polarities" means this over on that side and that over on the other side, and "one"—the one who speaks here and is spoken of and to (*this* "one")—very much in the middle. From one side comes a question. From the other side comes an answer. To a different question. Very interesting. Yes, and one finds that the poem is here in the middle also, a taut little rubber band stretched between two poles of the divided mind, its very tautness an indication of what it is about: sign of an interesting mind at work. One hopes.

Signification, also, of where one is. The only regions of any importance, one is tempted to say, are the regions of the mind (in that most general sense: what one feels, thinks, perceives, knows, etc.), but . . . who lives *there?* The mind, embodied of course, dwells always in some region not itself, which enables it to become, as even in the poem, one's concrete and touchable self. So that states of mind—to be real, to be interesting—emerge in the contexts of seasons, geographies, entire populations, the artifacts of a culture, or some part of it, in a particular time, a particular place. The poem as landscape, showing *where* one is. Or has been.

report from Cleveland

i have been there, you must believe me!
see this map, which i drew with my own hands:

the hills are green and the buildings black
and there are many peoples.
o so many peoples!
i know that one and that one and that one and that one
and many others besides,
who would be of little interest to you.

on the map you can see clearly
that this is the way i went there
and this is the way i came back.
the highways were not bad, considering,
the weather bearable.
there is usually plenty to eat.

nothing requires you to take all this on faith.
here's the map: go see it for yourself!

And manifestation of the self. Plato, one wants to say,
if you were afraid of poetry you must have been afraid of
people.(Such an attitude for an arch-romantic! But perhaps that's the only way to have a perfect republic: have
it perfectly empty, no polarities then. *Nothing* very interesting, in fact.) Let's face it, the danger wasn't (isn't)
what the poets might say but *who*—which perhaps was
even worse. No need to worry, really, about poetry per-
suading anyone to do the wrong thing (or, for that matter,
anything)—such worries being merely a confusion between language as rhetoric and language as manifestation
that has been with us lo these many years since—once

one understands that poetry is a showing, not a telling (and one learns early in one's grade school career which half of the show and tell routine is interesting). If the poem persuades one to anything, it's only to look at it, the poem, manifestation of the self, and encounter the who who is there, not the clarified mind of the ideal citizen in its ideal state, but the mind as it is: individual and representative, detached and embodied, expressed and concealed, beleaguered and victorious, open and impenetrable, displaced and at home, united and polarized at once. Who can see that and feel secure in the republic? There's no danger in art that stoops to persuasion, the passer-by (commuter, neighbor, survivalist!) can see the direction of the persuasion and judge his passage accordingly, but this other, this poetry, why, it boggles the mind, as they say—because it manifests the boggled mind. And after such knowledge, as they also say, what forgiveness?

☙

As in the fairy tale, as always, one (the youngest child, of course: whatever one's ultimate standing, there was always a time when one was the youngest child) finally takes up the challenge and, with the dual polarities of the self in either hand—one's skills and one's ineptitudes—sets forth on this most intriguing quest.

> the king appears on a platform in
> 'the garden of the singing rose.'
>
> he announces:
>
> 'there are enough trees with enough apples
> for everyone to have at least one.'
>
> this is no monarchy and we do not
> know where he has come from, but

we obey him all the same: he has
a ring, a mantle, an animal confidante,
a beautiful daughter. in short,

he is not here and we are,
so each of us sets out with
a different shade of red or gold in his mind.

☙

Polarities: what is inside one and what is outside. Gift
of one and theft of the other, poetry an endless game of
put-and-take, sharing—attempting to bring together?—
one's self with the world, and vice versa; Poe-larities, since
he surely understood: we are buried alive, inside one another. The polarity of poetry: the journey one is forever
beginning: poetry as the truly polar experience: a cir-
cumpolar navigation, in which, of course, one ends where
one began, but with, all the same, so much accomplished.
And so much still unknown. And the polarity, finally,
of the person and the poem, the experience of the coming
together of these polarities, as in this mostly stolen para-
digm:

before reading this, you are you
and the poem is the poem.

while reading this, everything
is somewhat confused.

after reading this, you are you
and the poem is the poem . . .

. . . only you are both
a little higher off the ground.

problem solving

the salad is on one side of the river,
still in the garden.
the salad bowl is on the other,
sitting beside the dressing on the table.
we are in midstream in a small boat.

consider:
we and the salad must not be in the boat together.
the dressing is non-transportable.
only a single crossing is possible.

moreover, the dog is in the water already,
swimming strongly, the tow-rope in his teeth,
and the current carries us sideways,
ignoring the green signal of the lettuce,
the red of the tomatoes.   now:

pick up your oars! in the next chapter
we begin to deal in multiple unknowns.

⚲

slideshow

these are the badlands, which i have carved
to resemble the deep erosions of travel.

this is a geyser: the moist question
it keeps asking is both yours and mine.

and here are the rockies, arched with loneliness,
great glacial lakes chilling their laps.

this is a rain forest, myself beneath the moss,
everything green and nothing moving.

this is the ocean but must be the wrong ocean:
these frozen waves don't move from you to me.

this is the desert. the desert speaks for itself.

16
Alvin
Greenberg

and this is a metaphor and not
the desolate town in the middle of nowhere it seems:

above it stands the sun, that harsh projector,
waiting for the moon to move before it again

cooling the long, western glare of summer.

♀

in poems begin responsibilities

looking through old poems for the mole
on your right breast, I miss

an unexpected step—and the world trips,
spilling the green tray of summer.

spaceship july: everything floats,

gravity looking on like an uninvited guest,
clasping and unclasping its thin hands.

take a lesson in weightlessness:

turning the world upside down,
looking for your mark in the spaces

between the ordered stanzas of my life,
selves i never knew i had

drift around me in the shadow of the moon.

at night i lie awake beside them,
tucked in between my lines and yours,

working out the meaning of 'equilibrium'.

THE PRESERVATION OF SELF IN EVERYDAY LIFE

*Alvin
Greenberg*

dream 1

the number of lives in my life
is exceedingly many, and the colors
that glow in their fur
not to be lost sight of in the twilight,

and the days of the week of their comings
and goings remembered,

and promises made to them and
promises they have promised to keep

and the particular song that each one sings
from the long catalogue of their music

in my head.

dream 3: help from the gods

i need:

a dog as big as the moon
and stupid enough to challenge the gates of hell.

they say:

'your wish is granted:
                    good luck

at the other end of the leash.'

refrain

we all have black shadows:

i wrap myself up in mine
and disappear.

dream 4

more snow than anyone has ever seen before:

snow drifting against the top storeys
of all the office buildings

snow filling in the whole mississippi valley

and i keep saying, 'i'm not
cold, i'm not cold' and let myself go drifting

deep into the valley between your breasts.

the unexpected

the neanderthal of my own past
hunkers down with a bone in his hand
in the shadow of a rock whose exact location
only i know.

he waits to see if i dare to pass that way.

dream 9

the neighbors have hung out shingles
to identify their professions

but i can't read them.
they are committed to significant strategies,
according to the seasons,
in their garages and backyards

but it's all i can do to keep mine clean.

they converge in lumbering trajectories
on a spot marked x

that i can't bring myself to step aside from
seeing how at the distance of a few feet

they explode softly

and the air around me lights up with real people.

conservation

even the golden eagle,
who can outfly me any day of the week,
has protection under federal law

though there are fewer of me than him.

dream 12

voices that sang barroom songs and brayed
and voices chanting over small objects at dawn
voices that spilled out into the rain

voices that cradled the snow
voices that lay dry and cracking in the streets

a pair of voices saying yes and no, yes and no

voices that spoke of other things, other things
a voice that failed to become a voice at all

a voice that could speak in no
other voices than its own and one
that could only speak in other voices

a voice where there were no listeners. none
and the last voice of all, saying go forth

and do as little damage as possible.

little song

bone on shadowy bone goes
crack: this dark eclipse of music

has ears and fur itself, and's
what i've made to travel with.

dream 17

we enter another world now,
in which time moves less quickly:

where the trajectory of a bullet
is a dotted line whose end we can all see
and step aside from

where the moment of our waking together
goes on and on

and we live recklessly inside it.

envoi

in this land i am the native *and*
the anthropologist.

between us on the dirt floor
burns a small fire, called

'the "rightness" of my own ceremonies.'

Alvin
Greenberg

miscellaneous landscape

the cyclist who lifts the turtle from the road,
carrying home the orange and black shell
that the sunday traffic would soon have crushed,

the lake from which that turtle crept ashore,
haze of the city from which the cars have come
and implications of prairie in the uncut grass:

the poem is simply what is seen, lending
some coherence to all that moves through it,

an order for the fragments of the visible.

like the paired sight of binoculars, its lines
converge by design on the most distant object:

see those hills? close up, nothing's left of them
but figures, bushes, weed clumps: the landscape,

face to face, no longer a landscape at all.
something happens. the poem's what strictly seen.
don't mistake coherence for life. that turtle,

rescued from onrushing cars in the first stanza,
is killed, before the last, perhaps by a dog,
in the night, between the lines. no one saw it.

can you then, given the poem as it is, hold
these powerful binoculars steady in your hands?
will you rest them on my shoulder, leaning softly

against my back? can you, leaning into me, hold
these fragmented landscapes steady in your mind?

the poem is simply who is seen: you, leaning
your whole body into this dense chaos of mine.

landscape: *the prairie*

23
Alvin
Greenberg

it's the great american failure,
like esperanto: no one speaks it anymore.

it was the language of dreams,
forgotten as soon as the dreamer awoke,
its slow rhythms chopped up into useful terms:

eat, buy, plant, build, kill, sell, go . . . .

like grass we didn't plant it thrusts up now
through cracks in the new sidewalk.

this always happens, so we can ignore its meaning,
turning it into an academic exercise:

we teach it to schoolchildren like latin,
and all that sticks is the flat phrase meaning

dead, dead, dead, dead, dead, dead . . . .

we teach them how to stand outside in the evening,
watering the sidewalk, not the grass,

and when they grow up and it becomes midnight
and when they pace the dark house listening
to the soft accents of their children breathing

and hear the muffled breath of the prairie
picking like dreams at all their locks,

they think: we know your meaning, we do,
what we don't know is . . . what you refer to.

24
Alvin
Greenberg

there are three totally different poems here.

1.

the first in which the water rises and falls,
with the season, a small lake, like myself,
with no outlet, a bathtub without a drain:

whatever happens fills it to the brim.

in mid-summer you can just see, above it,
the fine haze of evaporation: experience
surfacing vaguely over it like a poem.

2.

a second which vibrates with the flight of ducks,
whose surface records what ducks have done to it:

the scars of the long wakes of ducks landing,
the snags of ripples closing over ducks diving,
froth torn up by the wingbeat of ducks ascending.

this is a badly damaged lake. with icy lines
it tries to close over itself, like a poem.

3.

and a third in which the ice goes slowly out
and the water warms to me. the ice goes out.

it abandons the shore. wind directs its retreat.
ice darkens to the water it becomes. the lake

is a lake again, waters risen with the season.
we are full, full, full, full, full, full . . .

no outlet? we'll simply overflow, like a poem.

landscape with nesting figure

see that man in the corner, behind the sofa,
gathering twigs and bits of string?

like a startled pheasant his delusion
whirrs up among canapes and cocktail glasses,

his presumption of comfort a target for laughter
among these, his own sophisticated guests.

he himself remains below—building, building—
and as dull at recognizing natural enemies

as a creature prepared to become extinct.
he's yesterday's bird—still presentable

but shabbier than anyone else at the party.
wearing the brown suit of his determination

he wedges into the chinks of the final stanza,
as if it were a real world with a real future,

the toothpicks, olive pits, and peanut shells
you've been so busy hurling at him here.

Alvin
Greenberg

26
Alvin
Greenberg

the air is so heavy with rain
even taste and odor grow soggy.
when i read from this damp card

the recipe for hungarian goulash,
no ingredients announce themselves.
weather dominates everything.

there's a cloud in the west
black as a full eclipse of you
that says: 'night, go hungry,

power lines all fall down now,
what do you need, what need?'
we pass, in silence, pots, salt,

fumbling among knives and meat
with each other's fingers.
what we do says what we need.

we have to eat and eat and eat:
our bodies thunder appetite
no matter what the weather says.

perhaps it is night already
and we are cooking in the dark,
practicing for blindness.

foreign landscape

we who move out of our dreams across the dark
borders of night, we who smuggle our dreams
in the hollow chambers of our hearts, we

whose every gesture is stuffed with contraband,

whose eyes violate the security of the awakened
and threaten to devalue brick and stone . . .

does the citizen feel cheated who buys from us,
overpaying for what should have been his own?

he hears us ticking loudly in the night, thinks:
we walk the streets like ordinary citizens.

well, let no one be fooled if we are seen

strolling hand in hand at the hour of promenade
or sharing, in the open restaurant on the square,
tastes of each other's food. each other.

and let no one be fooled by the way we speak
the language, or by our casual manner
with the currency and politics of daily life.

we are always in a foreign country. this landscape
no one knows. evenings, in the park we sit,

delicate containers of dreams lethal as bombs.
when it grows dark we close our eyes: go home.

27
Alvin
Greenberg

28
Alvin
Greenberg

the world is studded with signposts: this
woman, for example, alight with direction,
one corner of her mouth turned up, the other
down, solidly imbedded between these lines.

why, the traveler who pauses here is himself
a sign, as his children are signs, who mingle
in the crowd at this confusing crossroad.

and the open window in the house by the road
is a sign. and the lake is a sign. and you
are a sign. and you and you. and the container

of all these signs itself a sign which says:

we must all identify each other correctly,
devouring the contradictions of stop and go,
planting ourselves along the dangerous curves.

only then can we decipher our own directions,
reading 'everything leads to everything else.'

landscape: *the mind*

everything here is created purely from memory:

29
Alvin
Greenberg

the grass an improbable green and mountains
in the even, purple rows of a child's drawing.

nothing moves. the sky is carefully arranged,
the tree dead center. august stills the birds.

it is all done by mirrors, in which everything
belongs to something else: except that arm,

lying still there, the long fingers curved
across the pale breast, which i assign to you.

nothing moves here. neither the iron furniture
of memory—lawn chairs by a grey-green river—

nor the rain forgotten in the distant clouds.
the sky colorless, the tree still, dim thunder

of possibility as faint, behind the mountains,
as the mark of your fingernail on your breast

when i raise your hand in mine. nothing moves,
yet the mark fades. your skin turns as smooth

as the memory of the future, creating itself
like clouds, unseen, like the mirrors in which

i turn this poem, once pure and still as memory,
into you, only you moving across this landscape

i inhabit like a man holding his breath, forever.

ultimate landscape

this is the landscape after making love.
here the earth throbs like the pulse in your neck,
a miniature in which everything resides.

and what's outside it? anyone there who speaks
the language of lakes and hills, or turns
the great machinery of memory toward the future,

detecting its quick, erotic pulse?

here, in miniature, in the corner, we reside.
no tools but ourselves do we have
for chipping away at the firm container of the frame.

the landscape's simply who is seen.

well, like that quick, erotic pulse in your neck,
the earth throbs beneath us as we work.
everything joins us here at the edge.

and when the borders have been crossed at last,
when the loud ticking of dreams disturbs the future,
when speech and the unspeakable reside together

and memory begins to create itself anew: everything
here will spread quickly outward, this landscape
enlarge upon the throbbing silences,

and there will be no container for this thing.

BIBLIOGRAPHY OF POEMS PUBLISHED

A. Books

The Metaphysical Giraffe. New Rivers Press. New York. 1968.
The House of the Would-be Gardener. New Rivers Press. New York. 1972.
Dark Lands. Ithaca House. Ithaca, New York. 1973.

3 1
Alvin
Greenberg

B. Magazines

ritual luncheon	*Penny Poems*	no.86 (1959)
departure in a strange dream	*Poetry Dial*	v.1 (1961), 11
in the beginning	*Poetry Northwest*	v.2 (1962), 37
if winter comes . . .	*El Corno Emplumado*	no.17 (1966), 120
an impromptu home puppet show reality, with mirrors	*El Corno Emplumado*	no.19 (1966), 90-92
the basket remnant, auction, end-of-season sale poem	*Minnesota Review*	v.7 (1967), 211-213
new years eve 1966	*Poetry Northwest*	v.9 (1968), 17-18
the black jew structural flaws ave atque vale	*December*	v.10 (1968), 48-49
dark land/black poems poem of the box skin diving knowing what it is you say you are	*El Corno Emplumado*	no.25 (1968), 63-65
arhythmia the past and the future	*So. Florida Poetry J.*	v.1 (1968), 11-12
one who doesn't like games an anniversary lost in travel	*Sou'Wester*	v.1 (1968), 56-57
curb your dog sat a.m. family love affair	*Epoch*	v.17 (1969), 148

1st principle of aerodynamics	*Yes*	v.1 (1971), 34
directions	*North Stone Review*	v.1 (1971), 39
the preservation of self in everyday life	*Antioch Review*	v.31 (1971), 224-234
climate of change	*Fragments*	v.1 (1971), 27
house of the would-be gardener: #4	*Perspectives*	v.16 (1971), 263
prayer for a lost sense egg dream	*December*	v.13 (1971), 76
american cookery a new astronomy a bestiary of domestic animals	*New: American and Canadian Poetry*	no.16 (1971), 48-49
house of the would-be gardener: #2	*Hiram Poetry Review*	no.11 (1971), 10
agate hunting at two harbors	*Epoch*	v.21 (1971), 139
october at mocassin lake	*Antioch Review*	v.31 (1971), 332
house of the would-be gardener: #3, 5	*Ohio Review*	v.13 (1972), 18-19
ode to duty	*Latitudes*	v.2 (1972), 62
political cartoon command performance	*Centennial Review*	v.16 (1972), 258-259
inland sea	*Quartet*	no.39/40 (1972), 41
the time machine	*The Little Magazine*	v.6 (1972), 66
special delivery	*Akademi*	v.6 (1972), n.p.
last things grand tour houdini at the gates of hell	*American Review*	no.16 (1973), 79-81
spring song daedalus en famille house of the would-be gardener: #6	*Dacotah Territory*	no.4 (1973), 46-48

visitation	*Kansas Quarterly*	v.5 (1973), 25
directions dining out	*Poetry Northwest*	v.13 (1973), 40-41
problem solving	*Iowa Review*	v.4 (1973), 11
subdivision	*Epoch*	v.22 (1973), 324
status negative	*Agni Review*	(1973), 13
poem with obvious title	*Seneca Review*	v.4 (1973), 40-41
slide show	*Seneca Review*	v.4, (1973), 18

C. Anthologies

traveling man ceremony october at mocassin lake	*West of Ely*. New Rivers Press. New York. 1968.
american cookery	*The Sensuous President*. New Rivers Press. New York. 1972.
dream 17 envoi	*Toward Winter*. Latitudes. New York. 1972.

Alvin Greenberg lives and writes in St. Paul, Minnesota, where he is a member of the Department of English at Macalester College. He is married and has three children. Besides being a poet, he is the author of many published short stories and two published novels, the most recent of which is GOING NOWHERE.

Burton Hatlen Interview of George Chambers, December, 1973

Credit: The poem in this interview by Burton Hatlen was published in *Onan*.

Biographical note: Burton Hatlen is Associate Professor of English at the University of Maine.

H. You move back and forth between prose and verse without making too much distinction between the two. Do you think of some of the stuff you're writing as prose poetry? Is this in your mind a distinct poetic form?

C. Here's *an* answer. I'm lazy and not all that convinced that writing makes much of a difference, but it is something I find I end up doing. So for me the first draft has to be the final draft, the one I send out to the editor of the *Hinckley Astonisher*, or *Green Banana*. What I roll through the typer is "writing"; whatever anyone else may call it. It is slow work, a matter of close attention to words going on, getting laid down. I read it, I sound it aloud, I shove it to the right, or I follow it. Other things, "intentions," are also present. A common one has to do with length. Let's say to make something go 20 pages, or 365 pages, or to the bottom of the page. Or to type for an hour. My favorite intention is to sit on the foam and let it come forth, playing with it as it goes along. Little Mozart let me whistle you a tune.

H. You don't feel there's a significant difference in language between your fiction and your poems?

C. Maybe. I guess if I'm obeying some intention, say to make a long thing, the language, the sentences, are apt to be more relaxed. I may even describe the pattern of the rug the lady is working her puzzle on, but I find I get off that fast. Description you know, unless it is really *presenting,* is such dull slow stuff: to the left there are . . . up above one may notice. I mean who cares what color her eyes are?

H. When I'm writing poetry though, I find myself thinking a great deal about the line break. It seems to me that decisions as to the line break are the most important decisions I make. Do you feel that?

C. Yes. I see it in your work, the care, the difference it makes. If I'm writing a poem that has lines, then I think I watch first the line, then where it stops. A matter of the sound I think, wanting it to feel-sound "right." But, to be accurate, look, there's what I think I'm doing and what I do. Most of the time the line stops because it does. I mean, Burt, I don't think generally there's all that much care taken.

H. Why did you adopt a pseudonym?

C. Things happen, then we supply "reasons" for them. One day I was making these poems and they were by this Jirac Disslerov fellow, a truck gardener in Ljubljana. The name came to me, his name, and I signed it, perhaps was "assigned" it by the Powers. But then, I've been writing his work for seven years now, "reasons" occured. I don't happen to think who wrote something matters very much. Paintings were not signed until when? the fourteenth century? Did Duccio ever sign his work? I don't think so. I mean here's a jar of my piccalilli. Does God sign the pickle? Can I afford the presumption of a signature? I get on the bus, I adjust my tie. Good morning pregnant lady, may I offer you my seat? Another reason: when JD arrived I was translating things, and so there was plenny excitement and traffic. Anyway, I liked the jerkiness, the feel, of translations. So I was, there I was, "translating" Jirac Disslerov, that tomato.

H. Perhaps you want to write a poem that feels like a translation because it gives you an additional ironic distance. You not only have the experience and the language about the experience, but also, in effect, you are introducing another consciousness.

C. That's right I think, and scary, since, what, the sense of manipulation . . . makes me uncomfortable . . . I distrust it.

H. Do you want to be an ironic writer?

C. Well, no. I mean ironies occur, eh? But I have no interest in manufacturing them. Irony is a way of understanding what's going on, eh, a way of making even bleak sense-order in the town dump. But it gets in the way, much as any ordering does. So much so that the subject becomes the irony and not the specific gull droppings on the hood of the 49 Step-Down Hudson. I mean irony is too sweet, too delicious. Dessert, hot fudge. But I'm in distrust of opinions these days, especially wholesale. Look, there's your poem about trying to listen to Bartok. This one:

IN A STRANGE TIME

Trying to listen to
Bartok while the baby stands
in the corner and screams and
Julie watches George
of the Jungle and you wash
the dishes.

                 And it
all falls apart.

Last night the German doctor
said the demons are
again among us. They are
in the walls, that we
can't see through.
"Yes," I said, "It's a strange
time, as we
learn to live without
hope."

Still, the music comes
in, the strings, percussion,
and celeste. We all
hear some of it. So
you make a cake, you write
"Luv" on it, with
maraschino cherries, and put
it in the middle of the
table. It is
St. Valentine's day. If
it matters.

That lovely poem . . . I read it again this morning in the bathtub before coming up here. Now for me the poem wants to stop at "in the middle of the / table." I mean the poem gets going, a slow accumulation of specifics, so attractively, what? invitingly, modest? You know, a *place,* an occasion, and what *that* may yield, as in that recognition "We all / hear some of it." Zow. I mean that is *steady, there.* But the rest, from "table" on, is, ah, so much less for me. What is it? Too easy a recognition? *Merely* ironic? I suppose. Maybe it is that it's too bald. That is, the poem is implicitly ironic, eh? So why insist on it at the end so? But you talk about it, it's your poem.

H. I have no inclination to be an ironic writer, although I like irony in certain forms. Nabokov, for example. And I can get really fascinated in a level of consciousness which in turn undermines another level of consciousness, and so on. But if I thought of the conclusion of the poem as ironic, I'd drop it. I wasn't intending irony there. Actually, I guess, when I wrote it the only thing I was attempting to do was explain why she would be writing "Luv" on a cake.

C. Yes, good. That seemed right for the occasion. But for me more powerful if unstated, let the reader decide. I mean irony is an interpretation of experience, eh? What I want is to leave the poem specific, let the reader make what associations-interpretations he will.

H. This question of regionalism seems to me connected to irony. I associate irony with New England. Do you think you have been in flight in some way from New England? I believe that all the unhappy people I know are living where they grew up, and all the happy people have managed to put some significant distance between them.

C. Well there is the fact of moving, I've read about. But where did I grow up? I mean Oshkosh was originally named Athens, so I must have gained an inch there, eh? And Peoria is listed in *Howl* as one of the holy cities, a mid-west Benares on Kickapoo Creek. Seriously, it is I think a question too serious to answer in an easy way. What I know is that I've done most of my work in the mid-west. In Wisconsin and Ohio and Iowa and Illinois. Now Maine. Is this New England? Does place matter? But one ought to stay where one is unhappy, eh? I mean that is a superior condition of the spirit. I was walking down Main Street yesterday and a car pulled to the curb. I could see the pretty knees of the driver and so interested in that casual way and she tipped out onto the sidewalk saying "Cookie!" Ah? He he he.

Returning
          he found himself
there, still   the very one
the same those who had remained
had needed him to be, his habit
intact they said   they said
which, he decided, they had need of
having died so much, stripped so
and so he needed to forbid them that
announce he had joined them
in their loss   that they were closer
than they would ever want to be

No,
    when I eat a bagel I don't think of my old girlfriend
Schätzie. When I drive by the house where I lived when
I was married, I don't think of her either, nor that pain
I was always making for us. Listen, when I look into the
sky on a dark night I see clear bright stars. I say, "There
they are, those bright stars!" Such a sight does not re-
mind me of my own insignificance. I intend to bring such
purity, such achievement, to the top of Tukey Hill when
the comet K. will be visible we all do hope and pray.
However, if I see a dead man, a sick man, a man with
tubes run up his nostrils cranked up on a bed, then I do
the lowland shakes, the ghetto jitters. And when I'm in
bed with you they all come before me, accusing, knives
glittering in the starlight, those women I forget, there
they are in the shadows, nightlight, dust. I sit up, pull
back the covers, motion them to join us, into my happy
bed strewn with inevitable flowers. When I'm a dead
man in my hearse they'll all be there, finally. Come at
last as they never could before.

She attacked him
in the alley with an ice-pick. As he turned, he saw the pick "coming down at me." She was disarmed. Later she told the police that the man she attacked, a news reporter on a local television station, "had said unkind things about her." Some months earlier, she attacked another reporter from the same station. At that time she claimed, after kicking the man in the groin, that he had referred to her as a hippopotamus on his show. I went for a walk this morning. It was cool and windy. At the intersection of Grolier Boulevard and Pleasant Street, a man asked for directions to G. Blvd. I told him he was standing on it. Hearing that news, he flicked his cigarette into the gutter menacingly and said, "No thanks." As I neared the apartment again, the clouds were as Shakespeare described them. "Hung be the clouds with black," he said. Yesterday in the NYT the Russian Solzhenitsyn said, ". . . I have almost come to love that deformed world." In my library I keep a picture of a famous golfer shaking hands with Goofy. I also have a picture of you surrounded with leaves. I think I'll have broiled chicken for dinner. It's Sunday morning. Lesson: if someone calls you a hippo, thank him for that gift. These times are so stingy even a word spoken in your direction is an act of generosity. Someone, after all, has given you a word. At least you can say that.

Yes, yes,

true enough, that is interesting to know, but is she married, is he married, are they married, how old and where live, that is what I ache to know. it is important to have opinion of course, but truth is statistics, and these days the soul requires them: stats, hard facts, numbers do not lie. I know a man who can quote the lifetime batting averages of every baseball player in the major leagues. I know a man who knows the stats on the tides in San Diego harbor a year in advance. I know a man who knows every rhyme in the English language. And so on. You see, with this information, we . . . But let me be simple. I mean if out of the blue someone you know happens to tell you that they love you, what on earth could you say? So what? How much? Wherefore? Of course not, of course not. So what you need is statistics. You need to respond *somehow* to that "I love you," to that imposition of that word set on your equanimity. Eh? Now the thing to do when attacked like that is to fire back immediately, he who hesitates is loved! Now, to this case in particular: Since "I love you" is essentially a statement about the weather, you might respond to it with, "Hmmm, looks like rain." and continue with a detailed forecast, which you should have at your fingertips, ready each day, the way you wash your teeth. I myself always quote the barometric pressure. Here is the formula: "I love you"—"Twenty-nine point four two and steady." (I'm not married.)

Model Diann

is wearing her tiger undies. I can see all the work there is to be done, she holds an adjustable plumber's wrench wrongly in her right hand. Her left hand is positioned to hold some object, but there is no evidence of it. Maybe it has been removed by air-brush. Maybe it was a bird that took off just before this record was made. Maybe it is another hand that has just been shakened, or is it shaked? Let's see now, if I shake your hand, you have thereafter the hand I shook, the shaked hand. Between her legs is light, still, almost stone in its palpability. One meets very few women these days without some light between their legs. I realize that sounds like something you might laugh at, something indecent. I know because it sounds that way to me. But what I mean is quite literal, the fact of how women are built through the hips this year. Model Diann, you want that "e," that completion and thus safety. I mean one wants the world one has made familiar to continue, as many comforting predictabilities as we can manage. I mean, as much as man may make yearning words toward freedom, who could, among us, handle it? Why else does the Portland Times print its daily predictions of the activity, the expected activity of the sun and moon and water in Portland Harbor? Thus we may look at paper Diann: we see what that hand is for alright, we know the work to be done. We know that belly-button is not there for nothing. I mean the tides are rising the sun is rising the moon is rising, right? You know what I mean, eh? Come on, toss the ball.

Spring

bring the body in
set it in a chair
feed it, let it look
again on an indecent spring
choking space of buds, leaves
squawking crows

I thought I was a singing
banana, what I thought
I heard was music

wondering how they'd live
this out, the good ones,
what they'd have to say

oh there is sun enough,
lying around the floor
with the dust, the dog
there is sound of dishes
being stored in the kitchen
& there is, counting the blessings
a lovely woman padding about
in slippers, clean air moving
through the rooms

when they asked the murderer
why he did it, he said:
because it is

tonight there will be
another disconnected moon
a wolf will howl
inside the cradle

the lady scolded me:
had I not noticed her
walking without crutches?

last night the President
blessed me & I fell
into a dead sleep

I picked up the dead dog
in the street, laid it out
on my front lawn, blood
seeping from its mouth
into the grass

my neighbor ran over to me
laughing: I am a nurse she said
and my husband is a mortician

I said a few words to the dead dog
I took off its collar and tags

if my daughter's horse were to die
she said: I'd cry until there were
no more tears to cry with

the girl wept in my arms
as cars went by, watching
she could not look at her dog
dead on the lawn
I gave her the collar and tags
she went home and took a tranquillizer

later in the day she came by
to thank me and tell about
her plans for the summer,
my old dog sitting in her lap

tonight is last night and tomorrow

I have acquired the following weapons:
a B-B gun, darts, a baseball bat,
a spring-loaded plastic rubber dart pistol

also, I have a saw, two saws, a hammer

I have a rock by the fireplace
I could hold it in my hand and
smash through a skull

also, I have a water-pistol

also I have a blues harp and a classical guitar

I have a football, boxing gloves

I have a long dog chain I could wrap around
my fist, thus making a mace

I have a bread knife in the kitchen
I could use that

                    May 3, 1973
                    Peoria

He was saving the poets . . .

He was saving the poets. Above him on a rock he could see gun muzzles dripping blood, smoke. One tried to run from under the ledge and fell, shot, water and tiny fleas spouting from his eye. He shouted, he held out his hand which seemed like a book. The man under the ledge was saving him, pulling him back under the rock, dragging the poet, it was easy. There, there, he was saying to the poet, to calm him, stuffing wads of pure cotton into his empty eye. You will lie on this special pallet I have prepared for you, he was saying, it will help your back problem. There was now more noise, as if artillery fire had commenced. When the man looked up he saw that scaling ropes were lowered down the rock face. To weight them, sausage and cheese, huge, the kind he remembered hanging in the delicatessen where mama met her lover the magician. A long, paraffin-coated cheese bumped in and out as it pulled down the scaling ropes which, now that they were closer, looked more like wires, the thick wound lower note wires on a piano. The poet was holding the wet cotton to his eye with the palm of his hand. He was angry, he was telling the man he had no instinct for form, he was telling the man that content was the real enemy, he was telling the man that in his next book he would make that enemy bleed. There, there, the man said, happy New Year to you my friend. Very soon now there will be blood sausage to eat and goat's-milk cheese too. He asked the poet if he had ever played the piano.

from *Amaranthus*

In good weather the old man sits in the metal chair on the lawn. In his hand he holds a tightly rolled newspaper. He receives what occurs about him without response. If a passerby on the sidewalk ventures a hello, his voice croaks out a reply.

It is Sunday. Across the street, people are coming out of St. Patrick's. A woman is talking to the priest. She looks about. She is happy to be seen talking with Father Damian. He looks about. He is happy to be seen talking with Mrs. D'Aubigny. The old man slaps a fly on his arm with his newspaper.

A pigeon is fluttering about the slate steeple. Bells sound from the loudspeaker in the steeple.

Behind the old man is the house in which he rents a room on the ground floor. A window is cracked. Strips of yellow masking tape hold the pane in place.

I am looking for an old letter in a box under the kitchen sink. A starved cockroach flops onto the linoleum. The roach is dry paper. The roach scuttles off.

The old man is sitting on a bus bench with the fat lady. She also rents a room in his house. They are eating ice-cream from the Velvet Freeze. The ice-cream drips off the cone. There is ice-cream on her dress. She is smiling her idiot smile. A bus goes by.

The old man wears a grey felt hat.

Do you feel lonely, did someone leave you, did someone not listen?

Have you given up, do you devote your life to objects?

Perhaps you save stamps?

There are wild shores, my friend, peaceful places where the ocean smashes on the rocks, where the sea anemonie is still surviving.

The fat idiot woman lifts her skirt. She is showing the

old man her panties. Her mouth is rimmed with white cream. She says, "Peek-a-boo."

The old man has forgotten.

The old man kills a fly.

It is hot. The old man is stepping from the curb into the street. In his hand, between his fingers, he is holding a strip of film, a piece of white lead-in. He is wearing his winter coat, his grey felt hat.

In the shoe store the young salesman is fitting a shoe on a girl's foot. His wish is that all pretty women would come in to have him fit them for hip boots.

Do you have a dog? Do you have a cat? Do you have a parakeet?

A bus goes by.

Every woman is your daughter.

Who is paying for your happiness?

The church is empty now. Through the open doors the altar can be seen. A newsboy is sorting papers on the front steps.

By the window in the old man's room is a table. On the table is an old wooden radio. Also on the table is a roll of toilet paper. Also the lid of a peanut butter jar. In it a piece of soap. He is seated at the table. He is resting his head. One papery hand is touching the radio. He is wearing his grey felt hat.

Tobacco.

The dog is pissing on the rug.

I have red wine, some whiskey. I could get beer. Come over if you can.

from *Kamadhenu*

SHE RISES ON AN ELBOW BESIDE HIM

If you die
this morning
you will burn
in funeral
pile of things
your clothes
books, hiking
boots burning
inside your
old Chevvy
and you on top
burning
on the roof

behold

POEM BY JIRAC DISSLEROV

you are in the water, you are swimming, and one says to
you as your arms and legs do what arms and legs do when
it occurs to them that they are in a watery medium: YOU
ARE SWIMMING SAMUEL and he uses the name you respond
to usually and you see it as a circle of loose letters that one
could organize in other ways than simply s a m u e l and
you find that fact very friendly and inviting, indeed as
pleasant as swimming itself can often be and as your friend
calls to you again to tell you that you are swimming, you
decide to ignore that description and then he says again:
YOU ARE SWIMMING SAMUEL and you DO ignore those
words and you find that you are sinking into that watery
medium and that it is getting harder to breathe and then
you are about to open your mouth.

from *The Iowa Review*

He is seated at the table.
Opposite is a woman (false teeth), a man (fake beard).
On the table is a leg, pink.
The leg is dressed in white netting, completely, toe to hip.
The woman and the man are telling him his future will
    be decided tonight.
They are serious. Their voices come as one, over the
    pink leg in the white stocking, into his ear.
He is smiling.
He is feeling like a hero.
He is feeling like addressing the crowds.
The woman is trying to find the best pronunciation.
    The man is being what he calls logical.
Your future, she says. Tonight, he says.
He feels worse, he wishes the crowd had not come. He
    pats the leg he placed on the table. He explains
    that the leg has been quite useful in his work.
    a marvellous teaching device, he says.
The man and the woman are speaking to each other.
He stands, places the pink leg on his shoulder. He
    smiles in their direction. He is walking away.

from *Crazy Horse II*

51
*George
Chambers*

52

George
Chambers

BOOKS

1972   *Chambersburg,* Northeast/Juniper Books, La Crosse, Wisconsin

POEMS

1962   "The Kingdom Of The Known,"
       "Perfect Order," *The Husk,* December

1963   "Our Town," *The Black Cat Review,* March
       "Excellent Work," *The Galley Sail Review,* Winter

1964   "Necessary Poem," *December,* Spring
       "Hog Time," *Northeast,* May
       "At The State Historical Society," *Forum,* Winter

1965   "An Occasion For Tremendous Music," *Sum,* April
       "Single Lady," *The Goodly Co.,* December
       "For A Worried Lady," *The Small Pond,"* Winter 1965-'66

1966   "To A Polite Lady," *Epos,* Summer
       "Indian Talk,"
       "Have a Beer," *The Lampeter Muse,* December

1967   "Come In Come In," *Quixote,* Spring
       "Captain Kydd In The Kitchen," *Quixote,* April
       "Dawn,"
       "Ground Fog,"
       "At Spring," *Wisconsin Review,* May
       "Late One Evening,"
       "Prayr," *The Poetry Bag,* Fall
       "The Punishment,"
       "Me,"
       "You,"
       "At Sammy's Grave," *Sou'wester,* Fall
       "Poem To The Gone Pumkin Lady,"
       "At The Table,"
       "In The Woods," *Cronopios 3,* August
       "Fall," *Poetry Review,* Winter
       "The Daisies,"
       "Werpo," *Experimentalist,* December

1968   "And Now," *Premiere 6*
       "Christmas In Georgia," *Runcible Spoon,* Spring
       "The Corner," *Sou'wester,* Spring
       "The Picture," *Colorado State Review,* Summer-Fall
       "After An Eviction,"
       "The Man Defines His Relation To Sylvia,"
       "The Poet And Indian War," *Northeast,* Fall
       "The Lovers," *Road Apple Review,* Winter

1969   "The Last Line," *Kamadhenu,* March
       "The Woman," *The Malahat Review,* April
       "Going Home," *Suction,* May
       "A Saturday," *Apple,* Summer
       "The Life," *Northeast,* Summer
       "Debris,"
       "The Introduction,"
       "Evening,"
       "Waking,"

"The White Hand," *The Poetry Bag,* Summer
"At The Hotel Word,"
"From The Treehouse, Tarzan, I Can See For Miles," *Wisconsin Review,* Fall
"The Man Defines His Relation To Sylvia," *The Massachusetts Review,* Summer
"I Want To Sell Buttons Forever," *Cronopios 6,* October
"Breaking Down In America,"
"Monday," *Sou'wester,* Winter
"Upon My Bended Spear A Monster"s Head Stands Bleeding," *Wisconsin Review,* Winter

1970 "Waiting,"
"Th Ghost," *The Back Door*
"The Company,"
"The Haircut," *Westigan Review,* January
"And I Was Down," *Baby John Gets Shot On His Way To The West,* September
"Untitled—'You are in the water . . .',"
"Delightful Pie," *The Iowa Review,* Winter

1971 "Untitled—'The red truck moves in the street . . .'," *December*
"Bush,"
"Laurel," *White Pelican,* Spring
"Roses," *Northeast,* Spring/Summer
"Roses,"
"Living More Intimately With The Moon," *Westigan Review,* Summer
"More," *Salt Lick,* Summer
"Les Objects Du Charme," *Occident,* Fall
"A Saturday," *Out Of Sight,* October
"The Example,"
"Getting The Message,"
"She Was Telling Me,"
"The Age,"
"Canoe," *Patterns,* Winter
"August 18," *Northwest Review,* Fall/Winter 1971-'72

1972 "The Something Man," *Kamadhenu,* April
"Sammy,"
"Thanking,"
"She Rises On An Elbow Beside Him,"
"Girl,"
"Singing,"
"Sunday,"
"An Occasion For Tremendous Music,"
"After,"
"The Voice," *The Little Square Review,* Spring/Summer
"Monday . . . ,"
"He is seated . . . ,"
"Help! A chld is pinned . . . ," *Crazy Horse II,* Summer

1973 "The Starry Night,"
"Untitled—'In good weather the old man sits . . .'," *Kamadhenu,* December

POEMS IN ANTHOLOGIES

1965   "Feeling Cold,"
"The Touch,"
"Up A Hill,"
"Summer Night,"
"The Day," *In The Late, Gnat Light,* The Art Association Of Cincinnati, Inc., Cincinnati, Ohio

1966   "Song,"
"Before The Enormity," *28 Poems,* Sumac Press

1971   "When I came back I saw . . . '"
"He was remembering his 'first love' . . . ,"
"The sun is up or out, I am . . . ,"
"I was giggling but . . . ,"
"All Night,"
"Primitive (after Jirac Disslerov)," *New Generation Poetry,* Ann Arbor Review Book

1972   "Delightful Pie," *Beowulf To Beatles: Approaches To Poetry,* The Free Press, New York, N.Y.

1973   "Once (after Kaveh Khatir),"
"Untitled—'You are in the water . . .'," *Breakthrough Fictioneers,* Something Else Press Inc., West Glover, Vt.

REVIEWS OF OTHER POETS

1967   David Kelly, *The Night Of The Terrible Ladders, Cronopios 2,* April

1969   John Judson, *Surreal Songs, Cronopios 6,* October

1970   G. S. Sharat Chandra, *Will This Forest,*
Sam Grolmes, *Moon Poem And After Oshkosh,*
James Stephens, *The Reason I Am A Creature Of The Waters, Northeast,* Spring/Summer
Peter Clothier, *Aspley Guise, Northeast,* Fall/Winter

PLAYS

1970   "Lyle And Avis,"
"Sunday Morning,"
"Papa And Co., Inc.,"
"Timmy Bower," *Assembling,* Gnilbmessa Inc., Brooklyn, N.Y.
"The Young Woman," *Transpacific,* Spring

1971   "Lyle and Avis,"
"Timmy Bower," *Onan,* January

Biographical Note

Currently on leave from Bradley University, Peoria, Illinois, George Chambers is teaching this year at Colby College, Waterville, Maine.

DEVILISH WINE

LIKE THE SANDS on the seashore, the hairs of your head, descriptions of poetry are countless. To Wallace Stevens poetry is "an abstraction blooded" and "a pheasant disappearing in the brush," while to Marianne Moore poetry presents "imaginary gardens with real toads in them." In the marvelous mixture of Sandburg it is "a synthesis of hyacinths and biscuits," and in the musing of Marquis "what Milton saw when he went blind." "Poetry is a centaur," claimed Ezra Pound: "The thinking, word-arranging, clarifying faculty must move and leap with the energizing, sentient, musical faculties." Frost considered a poem "a momentary stay against confusion, . . . an arrest of disorder." For Dylan Thomas a poem is a contribution to reality: "The world is never the same once a good poem has been added to it. A good poem helps to change the shape and significance of the universe, helps to extend everyone's knowledge of himself and the world around him." Suzanne K. Langer's pinpointing art as "felt life" embraces poetry too, and that's a taut summary. It reminds me of Lear crying out to blinded Gloucester on the heath, "You see how this world goes," and Gloucester answers, "I see it feelingly." Poetry is distilled significance.

The poet is an animal with the sun in his belly. He is one breed of the species cited by Luke the Physician as "a whole body . . . filled with light" (11:36). Rimbaud called the poet a stealer of fire. He robs the globe over which he roams, borrows from worlds overhead, extracts flame from his own viscera. He is essentially a maker—in their word for "poet" the Greeks embodied that concept, and the Scandanavians named him "word-smith." The poet is himself made to the image and likeness of God, and on the highest level of his operation he imitates the Creator. With language he puts flesh on ideas and feelings; to airy nothing he gives local habitation and name.

A practitioner of "the craft so long to learn," I am sometimes asked, "Why do you write a poem?" and I want to answer, "A poem helps me complete my being," but I usually say, "To find out what I'm thinking." Poets dig a lot of their imagery and experience from the unconscious memory, that bottomless ocean of man the dreamer. They select from this mass of raw dream stuff, sort it, assign it a logic and direction, give it words, offer it rhythm, music, movement, a particular shape. Stephen Spender once told me that he wrote a poem because he didn't find other areas of expression appropriate—painting, sculpture, architecture, music—though he had some proficiency in one or more of them. On a given occasion, Spender said, poetry seemed the right medium for what he had going in his mind and on his pulse. Sometimes no one is more surprised at the newly created poem than the upstart creator himself. My most invigorating shock in this regard was a sudden realization that it was I and not someone else who had written "Vendor"; the poem had sprung from a real encounter with a non-responsive salesman on a train, and it took this writing to trigger the mystery lurking behind the ordinary. To this day I do an unsatisfactory job explaining the poem to others. But should a poet have to explicate when the poem already in his best appearance? (Once at a lecture when one of my students asked Robert Frost why he refused to explain his own poem, Frost snapped at him, "What do you want me to do—say it in worse language?")

Every poet writes for himself; after all he is his own first audience, and he must please that audience. "When I have made a line that sings itself / So that I love the sound of it—I pay / Myself a hundred times," declaimed Rostand's Cyrano. But there's a charity to art—like Newman's charity of knowledge that calls for a larger audience. And so poets exchange poems, and they publish them in magazines and newspapers and books, though like the well-known rose petal flitting down Grand Canyon, sometimes the sound of the reception is not forthcoming.

Inspirations for a poem come any time—the worst climate for them is when you're bedded down for the night; the only sensible thing to do is to switch on a light, jot down the words, phrases, lines, ideas, then go to sleep hoping that in the definite dawn you'll be able to make order out of chaos. Poems can, incidentally, be written on anything—old envelopes are still popular, and so are tablecloths in restaurants. Frost wrote a poem on his shoe. I remember scribbling one inside my French cuff, another on my leg.

For what James Dickey has labeled "the backbreaking craft of verse," the subject matter is everything in the three worlds—man, nature, and God: from skin diver to calico cat to Red Cross Knight of Calvary, from milkmaid to comet Kohoutek to our white-bearded heavenly Father. Edith Sitwell took that a step further when she remarked, "The poet must necessarily occupy himself, through all his life, in examining the meaning of material phenomena, and attempting to see what they reveal of the spiritual world." Whatever is can be subjected to the act of language; there even the dull-as-ditchwater image can thrive in the green flowing springs of both poet's and reader's imagination. In poems old things become new and new things become amazing.

When Pound was asked what is the greatest quality a poet can have, he replied, "I don't know that you can put the needed qualities in hierarchic order, but he must have a continuous curiosity, which of course does not make him a writer, but if he hasn't got that he will wither." The poet of *Walden* said, "I am curiosity from top to toe." Still another kind of poet, Picasso declared, "Observation is the most vital part of my life, but not any sort of observation. I have trained myself to let nothing pass by: 'One never pays enough attention,' Cèzanne used to say, and I have made his word mine." So I warn fellow pilgrims heading for Helicon, Never be caught dead or alive without a notebook and ballpoint. Delacroix reminds us that Nature is one big dictionary and we draw words from it. There is something good everywhere our curiosity prods us. Chardin's "Nothing here below is profane for those who know how to see" is worth remembering enroute. We pity Wordsworth's Peter Bell who couldn't be a poet because "A primrose by a river's brim / A yellow primrose was to him, / And it was nothing more." But we are heartened by another Peter, the boy in Updike's *Centaur,* who gave early evidence of possessing a poet's juices:

> . . . It came upon me that I must go to Nature
> disarmed of perspective and stretch myself like
> a large transparent canvas upon her in the hope
> that, my submission being perfect, the imprint
> of a beautiful and useful truth would be taken.

Juices alone aren't enough to make a good poet, though. "Who casts to write a living line, must sweat," admonishes Ben Jonson over the centuries. The poet must tailor his poem to the shape that will wear it. This takes a lot of stripping, wrenching, pulling, ripping, and wresting, but passion for the right word will supply the personal courage. Housman said his big effort as poet was not so much to discover the right word as to reject the wrong one. Brahms also courted this practice in his art: "It is not hard to compose but it is wonderfully hard to let the superfluous notes fall under the table." The audience will acclaim the poet for what he omits. All poems need not have the gnomic compression of an Emily Dickinson, but athletic tightness and restraint must govern their conduct. This passage from "Clorinda and Damon" demonstrates what Andrew Marvell could do with only five lines of iambic tetrameter:

C. Seize the short Joyes then, ere they vade.
   Seest thou that unfrequented Cave?
D. That den? C. Loves Shrine. D. But Virtues Grave.
C. In whose cool bosome we may lye
   Safe from the Sun. D. not Heaven's Eye.

Marvell is a wonderful poet, and I always put him topmost on the list of safe ones for young writers. By safe I mean those who are hard to imitate—unlike, say, Thomas (who often enough terminates in diluted Dylan) or Williams (I confess *mea culpa* here) or Hopkins (Spender says he ferments in all of us). Shakespeare, the whole of him, is without equal. For diction and imagery, Rilke is splendid in his native tongue. During his later life Yeats wrote such clean, direct lines—the "please pass the butter" kind—that he is worth multiple readings. Keats of the Odes and the first version of "La Belle Dame sans Merci" should always be on hand. And Tennyson who had the best ear of all the English poets.

Only for record, and because I'm often asked who my bedside contemporary poets are, I'll recite a short litany: E. E. Cummings, for Ariel acrobatics and unsparing mischief; Marianne Moore, for architectonics and fearful scholarship; Wallace Stevens, for deep diving in the opaline seas; William Carlos Williams, for the ready word, the ready cadence; William Stafford, for straight shooting; Elizabeth Bishop, for "The Fish" whose eyes were larger than hers, "shallower, and yellowed, / the irises backed and packed / with tarnished tinfoil / seen through the lenses / of old scratched isinglass"; Katherine Anne Porter, for *Ship of Fools* bearing what must be the most beautiful writing in the world; and Charles M. Schulz, for day-in-and-day-out proof that earth's poetry is far from dead.

Although, according to Auden, "poetry makes nothing happen; it survives / In the valley of its saying," Kenneth Rexroth reports that the Chinese poet Tu Fu "has made me a better man, a more sensitive perceiving organism—as well, I hope, a better poet." To me that's a happening, in fact more than one. But my own best declaimer for the "inactivity" of poetry is my lyric "Recommendation: In Still-Early Spring." The girl for whom I wrote it eventually married the boy in the poem—one of my students "out of love" at the time of the writing. Though this isn't the true function of poetry—matchmaking—it sometimes functions that way. Because I'm a priest some people think I write certain poems to save souls. Not really. But I hope all my poems make souls worth saving.

Poetry also evokes special responses, extends unexpected rewards. For instance, I sent Marianne Moore my lines about a reading she gave in Chicago, a poem that started with the phrases, "Peacock elegant, the lady wore a necklace microphone," and went on to describe her as that rare bird with "dark jewels" and "a particular flight." She sent me a peacock feather. For a gift of my book *Love Makes the Air Light,* Auden regaled me over cocktails with a disquisition on the haiku, citing a number of mine for their allegiance to our effective but non-Japanese pattern of syllables, and giving me a lesson from his own recent haiku on how to break the strict 5-7-5 pattern, making the seventeen syllables better "fit" our language. One other cherished response was from the fisherman who inspired my "Riverman": he was so taken with the word-portrait that he gave me two of his treasures—a piece of driftwood with a walnut wedged in it, and the skeleton of a young gar. Then, from time to time, just because you are a poet some particularly sensitive friend or fan will present a token of regard: in my collection are bottles of dirt from the graves of Shelley and Keats, a box of carobs, stones from Walden Pond, some silver cocktail picks made by Mexican children (from Katherine Anne Porter), half a dozen Japanese sky rockets, and a kangaroo paw with a bottle opener attached. Feathers, flowers, pressed leaves, seeds, and incense sticks are perennials.

"Artists do the dreams for other people," John Logan mused one evening in my college study; "the curse of the poet is that he must dream publicly. Dream is private. Art is public." He then expressed hope that I would abandon my endless publishing in Catholic magazines, ghetto of "Catholic Poetry," and seek admittance to the secular markets where competition is keen and readership more universal. With his prodding, in 1956, I did gradually emerge from native Catholic territory to do my open-air dreaming in regions beyond. I never considered the dreaming a curse, but I've often reflected on the courage it takes to spin the spider threads of poems and hang them in plain view of just any passerby. Those threads are my guts.

Besides Logan, I have had God's plenty when it comes to friendly encouragement. Marianne Moore's "summaries" of my books and her critique of individual poems have been exhilarating. And when she was poetry editor of *The Nation,* Denise Levertov felt it was she who had "discovered" me, as she put it; she printed some of my poems there and she persuaded Norton to take my third book, *Love Makes the Air Light*—she was official reader of the manuscript, and no poem got in without her blessing. But every poet has more than two or three "patrons" like these; to enumerate all of mine, God wot, would be the sin of name-dropping.

For my own banner I've inscribed George Eliot's cadence, "Love is the word of all work." Through my poems I try to incarnate spiritual reality and spiritualize or humanize material reality. Engaging in this transfiguration of matter keeps me aware that my gift is from God. Any poet would be a bonehead to claim otherwise. The one thing our poems must do, as Auden said, is to praise all they can for being and happening. One of my students thought Augustine's *vinum daemonum* a livelier characteristic of poems, and he translated it "devilish wine." I like that too.

MY FATHER'S TRUNK

The soft grainy light of our attic opened
my father's past a little way. His trunk was
a place where years were shut in him like the leaves
of a book whose title alone he displayed
—I wondered if it was mostly about love,
though other strengths were there pressing a vision
on my landscape. I loved the hunters riding
in coon-tail caps through the ornamental path
inside the lid—I knew by heart the clipping
how he bagged a timber wolf in some woods near
Farley, Iowa, and I sported the brass
knuckles and dangled the billyclub of his
sheriff days, I aimed the elegant pistol
at spider targets—the topmost color in my
first spectrum was the greenpearl of the handle.
Under the sulphur white shirts with hard collars
and their beautiful musty smell and the old
leather smell of razorstrop were keys to locks
I never could open; an oval locket,
sealed tight as a dream, carried I always thought
my mother's image. I tried never to laugh
at the ohio matchbox with the sewing
kit of his bachelor days, and though it was
hard to picture the big fingers threading a
needle, I once saw that hand lift a bluebell
from its tower and twirl it like a sparkler.
The letter in the blue envelope he had
never opened bore a script daintier than
my mother's exquisite flourish, and when I
left the blue flap sealed, ordinary breathing
avowed the silence but did not disturb it.
Stale flower smell on another clipping brushed
me like rain: "a knot of English violets
enhanced the heliotrope gown" his bride wore
at their winter wedding, before "a long tour."

And every solitary honeymoon
to the attic filled my boyhood for a while.

One day I heard the plunk-plunk from our chestnut
tree, the gang all pocketing them for our pipes,
small fry on the block playing stickball, the flash
and thrust of limbs. I sat cross-legged before my
father's trunk and the wilderness of myself.
Signs I found in the tenacious silence of
things: I was the black-footed ferret, juggler,
harlequin: I was a touch on the padded
stairs, a balance of milkweed seed, Picasso
performance. With this strange fine figure of man
I had been playing follow the arrow and
capture the flag. Outside, someone was calling
ollie-ollie-oxen-free, and I was free
as a robin, a sun print on a swimmer,
the detached brownleaf and the unfallen snow.
Slyboots of that giant of my childhood, built
so long of limb and entangled in those dark
lidded privacies, I was equidistant
to 'love that makes the air light.' Chip of his strength.

Love Makes the Air Light. W. W. Norton & Company, Inc., New
    York, 1965.

VENDOR

On the New York Central from Chicago to South Bend
I saw him—at first from the back—and mistook him for
the conductor. His uniform was weary and dark,
his railroad cap might have come off the ark, and his shirt
collar was officially white under the stone gray.
On his tin tray he carried among the gimmicks some
cracker jack & tomato juice (and I had to wince
after cataloging them in files of Innocence
& Experience). He rattled up and down the aisle

of our coach a mystical 7 times—I counted.
Of his visagë children were aferd, very few
asking their mothers for a dime or two. Flesh sagging
from the bonework of his face and neck was the color
of frost bitten corn, his eyes had unhappy people
in them, and his drained lips crackled. The hands I had seen
before, on Halloween or in a home doctor-book
a boy will sneak through. He was hunched, rickety. And true.
(Little use to bury my head in Wolfe's epic of
the Angel—I strayed away from that confessional,
unable to put my ear by the stick crossed window
and help a man/boy say his fable.) The vendor held
me: I could feel him as a poem or candle-end.
So I was rather glad when we pulled into South Bend.

That night I took a cold shower and tried to send him
down the drain. I had enough ghosts of my own for bedfellows anyway, and would prefer sleeping with *them.*
But I didn't. I kept buying cans of tomato
juice which I poured into half filled waterpots of gin,
telling him a half truth about my fountain of youth.
When he wouldn't even wet his dryleaf mouth, I bought
a hundred boxes of his cracker jack, and I strung
the sticky kernels on christmas cord, though not too loose.
Round his neck I looped the noose, and hung him on a hook
in the skyblue ceiling of the 7th coach where kids
whispered innocent transgressions into the latticed
ear of a priest (whose wooden face never seemed to care
what else was toppling in their parish). Then I cried out
to them with a loud voice, and they came wide eyed and stared.
Before I died, I dangled till my skin burned to husk.
The grinning bones were left uncoffined. In single file
those children passed, the vendor leading them up the aisle.

The Small Rain. The Newman Press, Westminster, Maryland,

EVA PSALM

i

The old white beard of God is blowing
on the moon,
Old Glory shivers on a winter clothesline,
a spider eagle dozes in the dust.
Two dancers dance:
Tender ghosts of twinned Nureyev,

tipsy on the straight-up legbeat
puffing halos out of cocoa grit,
gamboling colts in dreamtime motion,
Keystone cops a little fat,
kangaroos in water mirror
landing softshoe as the cat:
their feet keep falling free.

ii

Shadow heads Omega-point.
Light is flowing like a beard.

iii

I-Thou.
We're on the moon.
Aye, Thou.

iv

Praise order, Jack-be-nimble,
praise *one small step,* Jack-man,
poke at the going embers of my life.
Hunt myself, Jack-hunter,
face up, Me-occupied.
Jubal, where's a harp, an organ?
Hang on a twig of language:
To that dance!

66
*Raymond
Roseliep*

Ring.

Ring around those fat thieves
gathering up the moon,
run the keyboard of my ribs,
Jack! roll the wick still higher.
Shake the earth grain guilty
from each wrinkled sole,
jump your blood past limbo
of restricted birds.

Spring, dodge, spin,
wheel, loop, ride.
Fly inside.

vi

The old white beard of God
is dancing on the moon.

Inside Outer Space. Robert Vas Dias, ed. Anchor Books: Doubleday & Company, Inc., Garden City, 1970.

TIMOTHY

My student gives me his six pound son
as he once gave me his bachelor's
essay on 'Childe Roland to the Dark
Tower Came'. I hold him as a sack
of plums, then tenderly as a man
with a portion of first folios.
Soon this weight in my hands will become
a bee of a boy carrying his
own honey as his father and as
I had done—oh, he'll strip, run to swim
dark waters darker than his pubic
hair. I hand him back to his father,
rummage my closet to see whether
I'd kept a horn that makes sad music.

Shenandoah. Vol. 21, #2 (Winter 1970).

WHEREFORE, NEW ENGLAND BOY?

Raymond
Roseliep

Tank top and cut-offs,
boy of summer digs
the dusty road to Verona
in thongs gold as his legs.

Fol de rol he's making
his harmonica sing
to plain jane sparrow,
hippie starling,

arcadian lamb
among "lions' teeth,"
connecticut angus
with bridal wreath.

Vernon to Verona
is a stone's
throw and songfest
in the marrow bone.

His heels are laugh dancing
toward spitpolish bright
moon and its fallen
ancient night.

Fol de rol his music's
undisciplined
as broken bell-pull
on the wind.

YOUR HAIR FALLS BLACKBIRD

68
*Raymond
Roseliep*

Your hair falls blackbird
on lotus shoulders
and rose berry breasts:
black as the young beard

of your boy lover
or nun's blowing veil,
more wave tangled than
the boat of Peter.

Your hair is haven
for his finger ends
possibly hiding
man and his heaven.

The Small Rain. The Newman Press, Westminster, Maryland, 1963.

TONIGHT, A MIRACLE OF AIR

Tonight, a miracle of air
you touch my dead grove
and the branches move
with excellent fire.

You sing in their marrow bone
holier passion
and sing a dimension
where ravens have flown.

I have loved you enough
for a night: and well
may the flaming apple
fall on my father's roof.

The Linen Bands. The Newman Press, Westminster, Maryland, 1961.

POEM FOR MARGARET

69
*Raymond
Roseliep*

Filling a jelly glass
with half-open
strawberry blossoms
was my afternoon business,
Margaret, my poem.
But you must hear of the wren
who stopped me short
with a water-
fall of notes—
*O-du-na-mis-sug-
ud-da-we'-shi,*
the Chippewas were right,
'a big noise for its size':
I watched him pick a hair
pin from the patch,
then make a wren-line
to his castle
of bleached cattleskull,
*O-du-na-mis-sug-
ud-da-we'-shi,*
I sang
and Chippewa-hopped
with the weathervane.

Here's my poem,
here's my interrupted
berrybloom
of small ablution
cups to fill a castle
or a single room,
and all
I wanted said.
I'll leave them
near the old brass bed.

Shenandoah. Vol. 19, #2 (Winter 1968).

MESH BELL

Night is quiet as a book,
snow jewel
brushes window's
honeycomb bell.

In that airy lattice
is the muffled note
matched
in my throat.

School bell, sleigh bell,
clock bell-tongue,
harebells for Leah
when we were too young.

Salvation
Army tinkling
night
sail to morning.

Night is book quiet,
honeycomb bell
rings the sea
like a shell.

THE SMOKE SMELL OF SPRING

The smoke smell of spring and your smoky hair
hum in the nostril,
that kid with the red cap fires a hardball
over the sun,
a housewife tinsels the branching clothes line
brighter than her sunburn,
a spider stubs a toe on rock
footlighting a ballet of violets.

In these middle years I hail my stance:
rise, move, turn,
a priest darkgolden,
oiled and wined for the dance.

*Raymond
Roseliep*

Love Makes the Air Light. W. W. Norton & Company, Inc., New
York, 1965.

WALDEN SOUNDS / *Four Movements*

I

Thoreau wakes, listens:
    bean sprout hacks away darkness.
Song locks in the throat.

Higher, Walden air!—
    dream stuff of dandelion,
        that beanstalk and Jack.

Pale blue butterfly
    lifting diaphanous skirts
        above skunk cabbage.

Ho, partner and thief
hammering the flour bin,
    carpenter titmouse.

Wood words shaping air,
    me here—can these draw Matthew
        from the countinghouse?

II

A green thumb of rain
    scrubs the frog on his heartleaf
    clean as a whistle.

Thumbnail on thimble-
    size blossom: half-moon of dirt
    crossing a white star.

Monarch butterfly
    throned on my letter, banning
    private matter—*pfft!*

This fife and drum corps
    riles my yankee blood—At ease!
    Fall out, mosquitos!

That fresh and tender
    bough of sumach is a fan
    falling—Henry, whose?

III

Wake up, Henry! Up!
    Artist whippoorwill, barn dance
    caller: ". . . *pur-ple RIB*."

Poets by a pond:
    man trilling, "tu-whit tu-who,"
    screech owl, "never bor-r-r-r-n!"

Unsaddle me, dream!
    Wind song and scale of cricket,
    outride that damn mare!

Wind and another
    hand once handled this oak leaf
    pressed in my accounts.

Country and town fool
    bumbling an old tavern tune:
    horsefly at my ear.

IV

What choir of hoot owl
   moans our unexplored nights—take
     care, Diogenes!

   Dirt-freckled poet,
   burlap mouse, hearth-born cricket:
winter bedfellows.

Looping frosty air
   like old home Christmas tinsel—
     glad rags of sparrow.

Wasp and mole bed down,
   Thoreau's firewood makes faces.
     The Ice cracks and whoops.

   Moon, find my bedroom,
the sweet Walden ghost tramping
     its pine-needle floor.

73
*Raymond
Roseliep*

SELECTED BIBLIOGRAPHY

74
Raymond
Roseliep

RAYMOND ROSELIEP, a priest of the archdiocese of Dubuque, Iowa, has an M.A. from the Catholic University of America and a Ph.D. from the University of Notre Dame. He was a member of the English department at Loras College for twenty years, and is now resident chaplain at Holy Family Hall, Dubuque. In the summer of 1964 he was poet-in-residence at Georgetown University, and he has given readings of his poems in colleges and universities. He received the Kenneth F. Montgomery Poetry Award from the Society of Midland Authors in 1968.

POETRY

The Linen Bands. The Preface by John Logan. The Newman Press, Westminster, Maryland, 1961.
The Small Rain. The Newman Press, Westminster, Maryland, 1963.
Love Makes the Air Light. W. W. Norton & Company, Inc., New York, 1965.
In preparation: *Tip the Earth.*
　　　　　　O Western Wind: A Book of Haiku.
　　　　　　Flute Over Walden.

PROSE

Some Letters of Lionel Johnson. University Microfilms, Ann Arbor, 1954.

ANTHOLOGIES

The Tidings Poets. Volume 3. Hildegarde Flanner, ed. The Tidings, Los Angeles, 1945.
I Sing of a Maiden. Sister M. Thérèse, ed. The Macmillan Company, New York, 1947.
Iowa Poems. Grace Noll Smith, ed. Duffy Printing Press, Des Moines, 1947.
Lyrical Iowa. Grace Noll Smith, ed. Duffy Printing Press, Des Moines, 1948.
The Poetry Digest Anthology of Verse. The Poetry Digest, New York, 1951.
National Poetry Anthology 1953- 1954. National Poetry Association, Los Angeles, 1954.
National Poetry Anthology 1954-1955. National Poetry Association, Los Angeles, 1955.
Joyce Kilmer's Anthology of Catholic Poets. James Edward Tobin, ed. Image Books: Doubleday & Company, Inc., Garden City, 1955.
Sealed Unto the Day. John Gilland Brunini, ed. The Catholic Poetry Society of America, Inc., New York, 1955.
The Second America Book of Verse 1930-1955. James Edward Tobin, ed. The America Press, New York, 1955.
National Poetry Anthology 1956-1957. National Poetry Association, Los Angeles, 1957.

Lyrical Iowa. Ruth DeLong Peterson, ed. Journal Print, New London, 1957.

National Poetry Anthology 1958. National Poetry Association, Los Angeles, 1959.

National Poetry Anthology 1960. National Poetry Association, Los Angeles, 1960.

Invitation to the City. John Gilland Brunini, ed. The Catholic Poetry Society of America, Inc., New York, 1960.

Fire and Sleet and Candlelight. August Derleth, ed. Arkham House, Sauk City, 1961.

A Selection of Contemporary Religious Poetry. Samuel Hazo, ed. Deus Books: Paulist Press, Glen Rock, 1963.

Of Poetry and Power: Poems Occasioned by the Presidency and by the Death of John F. Kennedy. Erwin A. Glikes & Paul Schwaber, edd. Basic Books, Inc., New York, 1964.

The North American Mentor Anthology of Poems. John Westburg, ed. John Westburg & Associates, Conesville, Iowa, 1965.

Of Poem. James L. Weil, ed. The Elizabeth Press, New Rochelle, 1966.

Poets of the Midwest. J. R. Le Master, ed. Young Publications, Appalachia, 1966.

American Christmas. Second Edition. Webster Schott & Robert J. Myers, edd. Hallmark Cards, Incorporated, Kansas City, 1967.

Heartland: Poets of the Midwest. Lucien Stryk, ed. Northern Illinois University Press, De Kalb, 1967.

Out of the War Shadow. Denise Levertov, ed. War Resisters League, New York, 1967.

Emily Dickinson: Letters from the World. Marguerite Harris, ed. Corinth Books, New York, 1970.

Harvest Hands. Sister Mary Samuel. S. L. Steffen Enterprises, New Hampton, Iowa, 1970.

Inside Outer Space. Robert Vas Dias, ed. Anchor Books: Doubleday & Company, Inc., Garden City, 1970.

My Music Bent. James L. Weil, ed. The Elizabeth Press, New Rochelle, 1973.

The First International Poetry Society Anthology. Robin Gregory, ed. Hub Publications Ltd., Derbyshire, 1974.

RECORDINGS

Lamont Library, Harvard University, 1961.
In preparation: The Library of Congress.

PERIODICALS

Poetry, beginning 1965 (excluding *Love Makes the Air Light*)

America (20 Dec. 1969; 23 Dec. 1972); *Annals of Iowa* (Spring 1974); *The Antigonish Review* (Spring 1970; Summer 1970; Summer 1971); *The Arkham Collector* (Winter 1968); *Arts in Society* (Fall-Winter 1967; Fall-Winter 1968); *Barat Faculty Review* (Jan. 1966); *Cat Fancy* (Sept.-Oct. 1971); *The Catholic World* (July 1967; Apr. 1969; May 1969; Nov. 1969); *Chicago Tribune Magazine* (18 Feb. 1968; 19 May 1968; 1 June 1969; 21 Feb. 1971; 17 Oct. 1971;

6 Aug. 1972; 3 June 1973); *The Christian Century* (5 Jan. 1966; 28 Dec. 1966; 8 Feb. 1967; 6 Sept. 1967; 4 Oct. 1967; 8 Nov. 1967; 15 Nov. 1967; 13 Dec. 1967; 3 Apr. 1968; 24 July 1968; 25 Sept. 1968; 29 Oct. 1969; 19 Nov. 1969 [poem corrected, p. 1501]; 3 June 1970; 20 Dec. 1972; 4 Apr. 1973; 19 Dec. 1973); *Commonweal* (17 Nov. 1967); *Continuum* (Winter 1966); *Counter/Measures* (#2; #3); *Delta Epsilon Sigma Bulletin* (Oct. 1967; Dec. 1968; May 1970; Dec. 1970; Mar. 1971; Oct. 1971; Dec. 1971; Dec. 1972; Dec. 1973); *The Echo* (Providence, R.I., 2 Nov. 1972; 9 Nov. 1972; 22 Nov. 1972; 21 Dec. 1972); *Elizabeth* (May 1970); *Encore* (Spring 1971; Summer 1971); *English Journal* (Feb. 1971; Jan. 1972); *Esquire* (Sept. 1969; Apr. 1970); *Focus* (Epworth, Iowa, June 1967); *Gallery* (Series Two, 1968; Series Four, 1973); *Haiku* (Canada, Vol. 3, #1 + 3; Vol. 3, #4; Vol. 4, #4; Paterson, N.J., Vol. 5, #1; Vol. 5, #2); *Haiku Spotlight* (Japan, 3 Jan. 1970); *HAP* (Purdue University, Spring 1973); *The Hartford Courant* (9 Sept. 1972; 25 Nov. 1972); *Hartwick Review* (Spring 1968; Fall 1968); *Hawk and Whippoorwill Recalled* (Summer 1973); *The Human Voice* (#28, 1971); *Janus-SCTH* (Oct. 1972; Apr. 1973); *The Lake Superior Review* (Summer 1973); *The Lamp* (July 1966; Sept. 1966; Oct. 1966; Jan. 1967; May 1967; July 1967; Dec. 1967); *The Literary Review* (Summer 1966); *Lower Stumpf Lake Review* (St. John's University, Spring 1967); *The Lyric* (Fall 1969); *Manhattan Review* (Vol. 1, #3); *The Minnesota Review* (Vol. 6, #2; Vol. 6, #3; Vol 7, #1 & 2); *Modern Haiku* (Spring 1970; Autumn 1970; Spring 1971); *Monks Pond* (Summer 1968; Winter 1968); *The Nation* (26 Sept. 1966; 3 Oct. 1966; 3 July 1967; 17 July 1967; 8 Jan. 1968; 17 Nov. 1969); *New Letters* (Fall 1972); *The North American Mentor* (Spring 1965; Winter 1965); *Northeast* (Spring-Summer 1970); *Northwest Review* (Spring 1966); *A Nosegay in Black* (Autumn 1966); *Poetry* (Aug. 1966; Feb. 1968; Sept. 1968); *Quartet* (Winter 1965); *The Quest* (Fall 1967); *Shaman* (Autumn 1973); *Shenandoah* (Winter 1968; Autumn 1969; Winter 1970 [poem corrected]; Summer 1971; Spring 1973; Spring 1974); *South and West* (Spring 1974); *Sparrow* (Dec. 1973); *Spectrum* (Fall 1969; Winter 1969-70); *The Tablet* (London, 13 May 1967); *Thoreau Journal Quarterly* (Apr. 1973; July 1973; Oct. 1973); *Time* (8 Sept. 1967); *Voyages* (Winter 1971); *The Wormwood Review* (#25); *Yankee* (Aug. 1968; Dec. 1970; Jan. 1971; July 1972; Sept. 1973).

Prose

Between the Lines (Milwaukee, Fall 1947); *Contemporary Poets of the English Language* (London, 1974); *The Critic* (Oct.-Nov. 1961); *The Human Voice* (#32, 1971); *The Lorian* (Dubuque, 15 Dec. 1960); *The Pflaum Review* (Dayton, Winter 1958); *Poetry* (Feb. 1966; Mar. 1966; Apr. 1966; Dec. 1967); *Poetry Pilot* (The Academy of American Poets, Oct. 1965); *The Priest* (Apr. 1949).

Poems

Beck, Robert. "Poetry Reading: Dubuque," *The Spokesman* (Dubuque, Summer 1959).

T. W. G. "On the Departure," *Focus* (Epworth, Iowa, Feb. 1967).

Heinrichs, Vincent L. "Of Linen Bands," *The Spokesman* (Dubuque, Vol. 60, #1, 1962-63).

Inez, Colette. "From His Life in Iowa Father Raymond Roseliep Takes a Morning Out for Poems," *Yankee* (Nov. 1973).

Keith, Joseph Joel. "Graduate," *Newman* (May 1958).

Keith, Joseph Joel. "Priest-Poet," *Four Quarters* (Jan. 1957).

Locher, David. "Dusty," *Michigan Alumnus Quarterly Review* (25 Feb. 1961).

Locher, David. "Telephone Conversation, 8:30 P.M.," *Cape Rock Quarterly* (Fall 1965).

Logan, John. "A Cloak for St. Raymond of Pennafort," *The Spokesman* (Dubuque, Summer 1959).

Minor, James. "Poem for Raymond Roseliep," *Delta Epsilon Sigma Bulletin* (Oct. 1970).

Runde, James. "To the Artist (R. R.)," *The Spokesman* (Dubuque, May 1964).

Ryan, W. E. "Lines for Raymond Roseliep," *Delta Epsilon Sigma Bulletin* (May 1970).

Southwood, Arthur. "The Confessor Afterward: A Metamorphosis," *Sponsa Regis* (Sept. 1964).

Taylor, Robert. "The Magister," *The Spokesman* (Dubuque, Vol. 59, #2, 1962).

Triem, Eve. "Carillon for Christmas Friends," *Delta Epsilon Sigma Bulletin* (Dec. 1972).

Vassilopoulos, William. "No Toybox," *Tri-Town Reporter* (Rockville, Conn., 1 Apr. 1973).

Zimmer, O.S.F., Sister Mary Honora. "From Carbon: Diamonds," *White Dove in the Oak* (Wake-Brook House, 1963).

Articles

Freese, Mildred. "Considering the Latest," *The Telegraph-Herald* (Dubuque, 10 Nov. 1957).

Hayes, Dennis J. "Conversation with a Poet," *Acorns & Oaks* (Davenport, June 1964).

Hayes, Dennis. "Magic and the Magician," *Today* (Oct. 1963).

Holscher, Stefanie. "Priest-Poet Bases His Life on Love," *The Harvest* (Dubuque, Sept. 1968).

Interview. "Father Roseliep Speaks of Poems and Poets; and Reads from 'Small Rain,'" *The Witness* (Dubuque, 28 Nov. 1963).

Keith, Joseph Joel. "Seven American Poets," *The Indian P.E.N.* (Bombay, 1 Mar. 1953).

Keith, Joseph Joel. "Spotlighting Excellence: An Appraisal of Eight Original Poets," *Mutiny* (Fall-Winter 1961).

Logan, John. "*The Critic* Presents New Catholic Poets," *The Critic* (Oct.-Nov. 1960).

Logan, John. "Poetry Shelf," *The Critic* (Apr.-May 1962).

Logan, John. "Priest and Poet: A Note on the Art of Raymond Roseliep," *Mutiny* (Spring 1961).

McDonnell, Thomas P. "The Poetry of Raymond Roseliep," *Four Quarters* (May 1961).
McDonnell, Thomas P. "The Status of the Poet in America," *The Pilot* (Boston, Supplement, 17-23 Feb. 1963).
McDonnell, Thomas P. "Three Unpublished Poets," *America* (29 Apr. 1961).
Martin, Dick. "Professor at Loras College Leads Three Lives," *The Telegraph-Herald* (Dubuque, 24 Feb. 1963).
Van Dore, Wade. "Thoreauhaiku," *Thoreau Journal Quarterly* (Oct. 1973).

Reviews and Notices

The Advocate (Melbourne, 14 Sept. 1961; 2 Jan. 1964); *The American Ecclesiastical Review* (Oct. 1961; June 1963; Feb. 1965); *American Weave* (Autumn-Winter 1962); *Archives of Internal Medicine* (May 1964); *Ave Maria* (19 Aug. 1961; 7 May 1966); *Best Sellers* (15 July 1961); *The Booklist* (15 Jan. 1964); *Books Abroad* (Spring 1962); *Burlington Hawkeye* (25 Nov. 1963); *The Capital Times* (Madison, 20 July 1961; 28 Nov. 1963; 25 Nov. 1965); *Catholic Book List* (28 Feb. 1966); *Catholic Book Reporter* (Nov.-Dec. 1961); *The Catholic Messenger* (Davenport, 27 July 1961; 28 Nov. 1963; 24 Feb. 1966); *The Catholic News* (6 Jan. 1966); *Catholic Standard* (Washington, 7 July 1961); *The Catholic Standard and Times* (Philadelphia, 8 Dec. 1961); *The Catholic Telegraph-Register* (Dayton, 4 Aug. 1961); *The Catholic Worker* (Nov. 1962; Nov. 1963); *The Catholic World* (Nov. 1961; Aug. 1964; Jan. 1966); *Chicago Daily News* (18 Apr. 1964; 19 Feb. 1966) *The Chicago Tribune* (9 Apr. 1968); *Chimes* (Notre Dame, Autumn 1961); *The Christian Century* (10 Nov. 1965); *The Commonweal* (28 July 1961; 8 May 1964; 8 Apr. 1966); *Connecticut Daily Campus* (2 Mar. 1964); *Cornell Sun* (Ithaca, N. Y., 7 Jan. 1966); *The Courier* (Dubuque, 8 Nov. 1963); *The Courier-Journal* (Louisville, 19 Nov. 1961); *Crest* (Davenport, 26 Feb. 1963); *The Critic* (Aug.-Sept. 1961; Apr.-May 1962); *Cross and Crown* (Dec. 1961; Sept. 1964); *Crux* (Notre Dame, 19 Dec. 1961); *Daily Times* (Davenport, 21 Feb. 1963); *Delta Epsilon Sigma Bulletin* (Dec. 1963; Mar. 1966); *Des Moines Sunday Register* (26 Nov. 1961); *Dominicana* (Fall 1961; Spring 1964); *The Dubliner* (Autumn 1964); *Duckett* (London, Aug. 1961); *Dyersville Commercial* (24 Oct. 1963; 11 Nov. 1965); *Elizabeth* (Mar. 1964; #9); *Emmanuel* (Oct. 1961; Nov. 1964; Mar. 1966); *The Globe* (Boston, 30 July 1961; 5 Jan. 1964; 14 Nov. 1965); *The Homiletic and Pastoral Review* (Jan. 1962; Jan. 1964); *The Hudson Review* (Spring 1966); *The Indian P.E.N.* (Bombay, July 1961; Apr. 1964; Dec. 1966); KTIB Broadcast (Thibodaux, 8 Jan. 1966 [typescript]); *The Lamp* (Feb. 1964; Feb. 1966); *Library Journal* (15 Sept. 1961; 15 Jan. 1964); *The Lorian* (Dubuque, 10 May 1961; 2 Nov. 1961; 18 Oct. 1963; 3 Apr. 1964; 12 Nov. 1965); *Lower Stumpf Lake Review* (Collegeville, Spring 1967); *Magnificat* (Dec. 1966); *The Massachusetts Review* (Spring 1966); *The Messenger* (Des Moines, 28 July 1961; 13 Dec. 1963); *The Miami Herald* (15 Oct. 1961); *The Michigan Catholic* (26 Dec. 1963); *Michigan's Voices* (Winter 1961-62); *The Milwaukee Journal* (31 Mar. 1968); *The Minnesota Review* (Spring 1962; Winter 1964); *The Month* (London, July 1964);

Morning Democrat (Davenport, 21 Feb. 1963); *The Mundelein College Review* (Dec. 1961; Spring 1966); *Mutiny* (Fall-Winter 1961-62; #12); *New Haven Register* (19 Dec. 1965); *The Newhawk* (Iowa City, ca. Sept. 1961); *The New World* (Chicago, 28 July 1961; 29 Nov. 1963; 24 Dec. 1965); *The North American Mentor* (Spring 1965); *The Northwest Catholic Progress* (Seattle, ca. Oct. 1961); *Notre Dame Alumnus* (Aug.-Sept. 1961; Feb.-Mar. 1964); *Notre Dame English Journal* (Vol. 3, #2); *The Notre Dame Scholastic* (17 Nov. 1961; 15 Dec. 1961; 21 Jan. 1966); *The Pilot* (Boston, 1 July 1961; 23 Feb. 1964); *The Plain Dealer* (Cleveland, 22 Dec. 1963); *Poetry* (Mar. 1962; May 1964; July 1966); *Prologues* (Sioux City, Advent 1961; Lent 1964); *Ramparts* (Vol. 3, #1); *The Register* (Denver, 26 Jan. 1964); *Renascence* (Fall 1962; Winter 1964); *The Rosary Magazine* (Mar. 1964); *The Sacred Heart Register* (Oelwein, ca. Jan. 1964); *The Saturday Review* (4 Nov. 1961; 19 Feb. 1966); *Savant* (Davenport, Spring 1962); *Sioux City Globe* (ca. 10 Dec. 1965); *Sketchbook* (Collegeville, Spring 1964); *Soconnian* (New Haven, 12 Nov. 1963); *The South Dakota Review* (Spring 1965); *The Southern Review* (Spring 1969); *South Western Louisiana Register* (ca. 1961); *Spirit* (May '62; Sept. '62); *Spiritual Life* (June '61); *The Spokesman* (Dubuque, Dec. 1961; Vol. 61, #1, 1963-64); *Sponsa Regis* (Jan. 1962; Mar. 1964); *The Sun* (Baltimore, 22 Jan. 1962; 13 July 1964; 18 Apr. 1966); *The Tablet* (London, 25 Nov. 1961; 11 July 1964; 1 Jan. 1966); *Telegram* (Portland, Maine, 9 Jan. 1966); *Telegram* (Worcester, Mass., 5 Dec. 1965); *The Telegraph-Herald* (Dubuque, 9 Oct. 1961; 17 Oct. 1963; 17 Nov. 1963; 27 Oct. 1965); *Threshold* (Belfast, Autumn-Winter 1961-62); *Times Review* (La Crosse, ca. 1963-64); *Today* (Dec. 1961; May 1964); *The Torch* (Aug.-Sept. 1962); *The Villanovan* (4 Mar. 1964); *Virginia Kirkus Bulletin* (15 Sept. 1965); *The Virginian-Pilot* (Norfolk, 27 Aug. 1961; 26 Jan. 1964; 5 Dec. 1965); *The Voice* (Baltimore, Spring 1962); *Washington Post & Times Herald* (31 Dec. 1961).

Biography

The American Catholic Who's Who; Community Leaders and Noteworthy Americans; Contemporary Authors; Contemporary Poets of the English Language; Dictionary of International Biography; A Directory of American Poets; Directory of American Scholars; International Scholars Directory; International Who's Who in Poetry; Leaders in the Humanities in America; Mondo Cattolico; Personalities of the West & Midwest; Who's Who in America; Who's Who in American Education; Who's Who in the Midwest; The Writers Directory.

COLOPHON

Fifty copies signed, 450 regular.
Times New Roman by La Crosse Composing.
Vicksberg vellum text. Casing by Frank Nekola.
Design and printing by the Sumac Press
of Emerson G. Wulling, La Crosse.